Fact Finders®

A Primary Source

THE WAR OF 1812

by John Micklos, Jr.

Consultant: Richard Bell
Associate Professor of History
University of Maryland,
College Park

CAPSTONE PRESS
a capstone imprint

Fact Finders Books are published by Capstone Press,
1710 Roe Crest Drive, North Mankato, Minnesota 56003
www.mycapstone.com

Library of Congress Cataloging-in-Publication Data
Cataloging-in-Publication Data is on file with the Library of Congress.
ISBN 978-1-4914-8488-3 (library binding)
ISBN 978-1-4914-8492-0 (paperback)
ISBN 978-1-4914-8496-8 (eBook PDF)

Editorial Credits
Brenda Haugen, editor; Sarah Bennett, designer; Wanda Winch, media researcher;
Katy LaVigne, production specialist

Photo Credits
Capstone, 13; Courtesy of Toronto Public Library, Item JRR905, 16-17; Courtesy, The Lilly Library,
Indiana University, Bloomington, Indiana, 1 (top), 7, 15, 18; CriaImages.com/Jay Robert Nash
Collection, 19; Granger, NYC, 23; Library of Congress, cover (bottom), Prints and Photographs
Division, 4, 11, 22, 25 (top), Three Centuries of Broadsides and Other Printed Ephemera, cover (top);
National Archives and Records Administration, 28, 29; Newscom: Picture History, 26; Shutterstock:
Everett Historical, 1 (bottom), 21, Oleg Golovnev, 8; Wikimedia: Francis Scott Keys, 25 (bottom);
William L. Clements Library, University of Michigan, 10

Printed in the United States of America in North Mankato, Minnesota.
102015 009221CGS16

TABLE OF CONTENTS

A NOTE ABOUT PRIMARY SOURCES

Primary sources are newspaper articles, photographs, speeches, or other documents that were created during an event. They are great ways to see how people spoke and felt during that time. You'll find primary sources from the time of the War of 1812 throughout this book. Within the text, primary source quotations are colored *brown* and set in italic type.

LACK OF COMMUNICATION

The War of 1812 lasted nearly three years, from June 1812 into early 1815. To the United States, it was the "Second War of Independence." To Great Britain it was an annoying distraction from its war with France. The war began over three major issues: trade, the kidnapping of American sailors, and concerns that the British were stirring up anger among American Indians on the western frontier of the United States.

Trade was probably the most troubling of the three issues. In the late 1700s and early 1800s, Great Britain and France were at war. As part of its war effort, Great Britain tried to stop the flow of goods into France. But France was a key U.S. trade partner. The British navy tried to prevent U.S. ships from entering French ports. This hurt the U.S. **economy**. People across the country suffered.

▷ American sailors fire the first shots of the War of 1812 from a ship's cannon.

economy—the way a country produces, distributes, and uses its money, goods, natural resources, and services

At the same time, settlers on the U.S. frontier faced increased attacks from American Indians. Some of these attacks came because settlers had moved onto Indian land. But many U.S. leaders believed that the British encouraged the Indians to fight against the settlers.

The third key issue involved the impressment of sailors into the British Royal Navy. Imagine being taken from the streets of your hometown by a gang of armed men. Then imagine being carried off to sea and forced to work on a ship. In the late 1700s and early 1800s, Great Britain needed more sailors for its war with France. Many of these sailors were taken from **port** cities in Great Britain. This was called impressment. Many people considered it kidnapping.

Often these sailors tried to escape. Sometimes they slipped away when the British ships docked in U.S. ports. Many of these **deserters** later joined U.S. ships. The British navy began boarding U.S. ships, searching for missing sailors. Sometimes they also took men who were U.S. citizens. One British captain said, *"It is my duty to keep my ship manned, & I will do so wherever I find men that speak the same language with me."*

port—a harbor where ships dock safely
deserter—a military member who leaves duty without permission

By mid-1812 the U.S. and Great Britain were trying to work out their differences. The British refused to budge on trade and impressment, though. On June 1 President James Madison told Congress that war might be necessary. He said that Great Britain's actions amounted to *"a state of war against the United States."* Congress moved to make that state of war official. On June 18 it voted *"that war ... is hereby declared."*

The timing of Congress' vote was unfortunate. Days earlier the British **Parliament** voted to change its policy on American trade. Parliament said that the British trade **restrictions** would *"be revoked, so far as may regard American vessels, and their cargoes...."*

It took weeks for the news to cross the Atlantic Ocean. By the time the message reached the U.S. it was too late. War had started. There was no turning back. What if the message had arrived earlier? Then the two sides might have continued trying to resolve their other issues. War might have been avoided.

▷ A letter from Albert Gallatin, secretary of the U.S. Treasury, announced that war had been declared against Great Britain.

Parliament—the national legislature of Great Britain
restriction—a rule or limitation

(CIRCULAR.)

TREASURY DEPARTMENT,
JUNE 18TH, 1812.

SIR,

I hasten to inform you that War was this day declared against Great Britain.

I am respectfully,

Sir,

Your obedient servant.

Albert Gallatin

The Collector of customs
for the district of
Newport

7

CAUSES OF THE WAR

In some ways Great Britain's war with France also helped lead to the War of 1812. By 1812 Britain and France had been at war, on and off, for more than a decade. Several other European countries joined Britain in fighting against French leader Napoleon Bonaparte and his **allies**. The United States remained neutral, not choosing sides. Although the country managed to stay out of the fighting, the war still hurt the United States. Both Britain and France tried to prevent the U.S. from trading with the other country. This hurt business with two major trade partners.

▽ Napoleon (on middle horse) on a European battlefield

As part of its plan to keep France from trading with other countries, the British navy stopped ships at sea. That included U.S. merchant ships. *"We consider a neutral flag, on the high seas, as a safeguard to those sailing under it,"* James Madison wrote to James Monroe in 1806. This was before Madison became president. In 1806 he served as the U.S. secretary of state. Monroe represented the United States in Britain.

The British, however, believed they had the right to search the cargos of any ships that might be trading with France. They also felt they should be able to search U.S. ships for sailors who had escaped from the British navy. They sometimes captured American sailors as well. In the years leading up to the War of 1812, the British forced 6,000 or more Americans to serve on British ships.

ally—a person, group of people, or a country that helps and supports another

The War Between Britain and France

The long war between Great Britain and France hurt the United States. Britain's efforts to block U.S. trade with France and its impressment of U.S. sailors into the British Royal Navy helped lead to the War of 1812. Britain's war with France also affected many other nations. Some countries fought on both sides at different points during the war. Following are some of the key allies for both sides as the European war moved toward a close between 1812 and 1814.

Key British Allies
Austria
Prussia
Russia
Spain
Portugal
Sweden

Key French Allies
Kingdom of Italy
Duchy of Warsaw (Poland)

9

One incident raised tensions even higher. In 1807 a British warship captain demanded a search of the USS *Chesapeake*. He sought deserters from the British navy. The captain of the U.S. ship refused. The British opened fire. Several U.S. sailors were killed or wounded. The British boarded the ship and captured four men. One was a British deserter. The other three were U.S. citizens who had been impressed into the British navy but had escaped. U.S. sailor William H. Allen wrote to his father, *"my country's flag [was] disgraced"* by allowing the British to board the *Chesapeake*.

Americans were furious. Some wanted to declare war on Great Britain then. The leaders of the two nations managed to calm tempers for a while. But this incident raised awareness about the kidnapping of U.S. sailors. As the kidnappings continued, more and more people began to feel that war with Great Britain might be necessary.

 the boarding of the *Chesapeake*

△ American Indians fought U.S. soldiers in the Battle of Tippecanoe.

The U.S. also believed that the British encouraged American Indian tribes to make war against settlers on the frontier. In some cases this may have been true. In other cases the unrest was simply a result of settlers moving onto American Indian lands. The frontier area covered Ohio and what are now the states of Illinois, Indiana, and Michigan. Tensions led to a battle at Tippecanoe in Indiana in 1811. Shawnee warriors clashed with U.S. forces. After a fierce battle, the Shawnee braves were forced to retreat. Indiana Governor William Henry Harrison reported that the attackers were *"finally put to flight."* But this battle did not end the bloodshed. Fighting continued between settlers and American Indians.

CRITICAL THINKING

Why might American Indians have sided with the British during the War of 1812?

Even after the War of 1812 began, the U.S. government was torn about how to handle the fight against Great Britain. Great Britain controlled Canada, which bordered much of the frontier area. Some U.S. leaders wanted to invade Canada and drive the British out. They believed this would prevent the British from meddling in frontier affairs. A few even hoped to **annex** part or all of Canada. Other leaders wanted to stop the war before major battles broke out. They wanted to negotiate for peace. Still others hoped that simply declaring war would cause the British to back down and accept the U.S. terms for peace. Instead, Britain was offended that the Americans dared to declare war on them. The British thought the issues with the Americans were minor. They did not believe any of these issues were worth going to war over.

Most of the mighty British army and navy were in Europe fighting with France. Even so, declaring war against one of the world's strongest nations was a risky move. What would happen next?

CRITICAL THINKING

How would fighting against France affect Great Britain in its war with the United States?

annex—claim authority over the land of another nation

American territory
British territory
★ Battle
Map shows boundaries of 1812

CANADA
(British North
America)

disputed

Maine
(Mass.)

Montreal

L. Champlain

*Lake
Ontario*

York
(Toronto)

*Lake
Huron*

Vt.

N.H.

New
York

Niagara
Queenston
Heights

*Lake
Erie*

Mass.

Conn.

Hudson R.

Rhode Island

Michigan
Territory

Detroit

Battle of
the Thames

*Raisin
River*

Ohio

Pennsylvania

New
Jersey

Delaware

Illinois
Territory

Lake Michigan

Baltimore

Fort McHenry

Washington, D.C.

Maryland

Chesapeake Bay

Indiana
Territory

Virginia

Missouri
Territory

Kentucky

North
Carolina

Mississippi R.

Tennessee

South
Carolina

Mississippi
Territory

Georgia

Louisiana

New Orleans

Florida
(SPAIN)

*Gulf of
Mexico*

*Atlantic
Ocean*

N
W   E
S

0   100   200   300 miles
0 100 200 300 kilometers

ENGLAND
FRANCE
UNITED
STATES

CANADIAN DISASTER

The United States was not prepared for war. Its army had only about 12,000 men. Its navy had about 20 warships. The British navy had more than 500 warships and well over 100,000 sailors. Its army had nearly 250,000 troops.

But the British only had 7,000 troops in North America. They were stationed in Canada. The British could also draw on **militia** forces and Indian allies. Fewer than 100 British ships were stationed near the United States. The rest of Britain's forces were involved in the war against France. The British used the ships they had nearby to set up a **blockade** along much of the Atlantic coast. It cut down on the amount of goods going in and out of the U.S. This hurt the U.S. economy. Prices of many goods skyrocketed.

The U.S. decided to strike quickly in case Britain planned to send more troops and ships across the ocean. U.S. military leaders decided to invade Canada. The goal, wrote former President Thomas Jefferson, would be *"the final expulsion of England from the American continent."* The United States also hoped that victory in Canada would convince Britain to quickly stop the war.

militia—a group of citizens who voluntarily serve as soldiers in emergencies
blockade—a military effort to keep goods from entering and leaving a region

a list of weapons, ammunition, and other materials at Fort Detroit, detailed as part of General Hull's surrender

Instead, the Canadian campaign ended in disaster. At Fort Detroit, General William Hull commanded 1,800 soldiers. He faced a smaller force of British soldiers. Aiding the British were American Indian warriors under the great leader Tecumseh. Hull panicked. Rather than fight, he quickly surrendered in August 1812. He thought he was doing the right thing. *"I have saved Detroit and the territory from the horrors of an Indian massacre,"* he later said.

That fall, U.S. troops invaded Canada at Queenston. They were defeated by a smaller British force. Nearly 1,000 U.S. troops surrendered. Meanwhile, U.S. General Henry Dearborn led another army to capture the city of Montreal. After a brief skirmish near the Canadian border, the advance stalled. Winter was approaching. Many of the U.S. troops were sick. Morale was low. Dearborn gave up the invasion plan. The war was unpopular with many U.S. citizens from the beginning. These failures to invade Canada lowered public support even more.

▽ Several buildings burned after the Battle of York, which is present-day Toronto, Canada.

Despite these failures, U.S. forces again invaded Canada in 1813. Many U.S. leaders still believed that driving the British out of Canada would be the quickest way to end the war. This time U.S. troops succeeded in capturing York (now Toronto), a major Canadian city. As they retreated, British soldiers set fire to the powder at their fort. A huge explosion followed. It killed and wounded hundreds of U.S. and British soldiers. Angry U.S. troops burned government buildings. Some homes were damaged too.

Soon after the fight at York, the U.S. army moved on to capture Fort George in Niagara. U.S. troops also recaptured Fort Detroit. But they again failed to capture Montreal.

When the war began, the easiest path for U.S. success seemed to involve driving the British from Canada. With that effort failing, would the entire U.S. war effort fall apart?

WAR ON THE WATER

No one expected the United States to do well in naval battles against the British. The British navy had many more ships and sailors. To help even the odds, the U.S. government licensed **privateers**. These speedy, heavily armed ships prowled the seas capturing hundreds of British merchant ships. They also helped the war effort by distracting British warships. One bold privateer named Thomas Boyle slipped through the British blockade. He captured 18 British merchant ships in just three months. He issued a statement that he was putting Britain *"in a state of strict and rigorous blockade"* with his single ship.

▷ Rules for public and private armed ships from the United States were explained by James Monroe.

Additional Instruction to the public and private armed vessels of the United States.

THE public and private armed vessels of the United States are not to interrupt any vessels belonging to citizens of the United States coming from British ports to the United States laden with British merchandize, in consequence of the alledged repeal of the British Orders in Council, but are on the contrary to give aid and assistance to the same; in order that such vessels and their cargoes may be dealt with on their arrival as may be decided by the competent authorities.

By command of the President of the United States of America,

Jas Monroe Secretary of State.

WASHINGTON CITY, AUGUST 28, 1812.

privateer—a private ship that is authorized to attack enemy ships during wartime

U.S. warships had unexpected success too. The most famous U.S. warship was the USS *Constitution*. The crew of the *Constitution* defeated four British warships. They also captured many British merchant ships. In one 1812 battle cannonballs seemed to bounce off the *Constitution*'s thick oak frame. According to observers of the battle, one U.S. sailor cheered, *"Huzza, her sides are made of iron!"* After the battle, the ship earned the nickname "Old Ironsides."

CRITICAL THINKING

How might the outcome of the war at sea been different if the United States had not commissioned hundreds of privateers?

▽ The USS *Constitution* defeated the British warship HMS *Guerriere* August 19, 1812.

U.S. Captain Oliver Hazard Perry won an important battle on Lake Erie September 10, 1813. Perry's small **fleet** outdueled the British fleet. After the battle Perry announced, *"We have met the enemy and they are ours."* Then he listed the British ships disabled or captured. This battle caused the British to abandon Fort Detroit. As they moved northeast, U.S. troops defeated the British at the Battle of the Thames. After these victories the United States again controlled Lake Erie and the territory around it.

As they made gains in their fight against France, the British sent more ships to America. They strengthened their blockade of key U.S. ports. Their goal was not *"a mere paper blockade,"* but *"a complete stop to all trade,"* wrote Lord Melville to Admiral John Warren. The blockade did not achieve that goal. It did, however, severely hurt the American economy. U.S. exports fell from $45 million in 1811 to just $7 million in 1814. As the war dragged on, more and more U.S. citizens wondered whether it was worth it to continue fighting. Perhaps it would be better to simply seek peace.

fleet—a group of ships under a single commander

BRITISH INVASION

France surrendered to Britain and its allies in April 1814. With the conflict in Europe ended, Britain could pay more attention to its war with the United States. In July British troops invaded Maine. The same month, British and American troops fought the Battle of Lundy's Lane near the border of Canada and New York. About 1,700 soldiers were killed, wounded, or captured in the bloody battle. Both sides claimed they won. According to American officer Lieutenant F.A. Sawyer, *"the enemy's bugle sounded the retreat for the last time, and our troops were left in undisturbed possession of the heights."* On the other hand, U.S. troops advanced no farther. That battle marked the end of American plans to invade Canada.

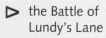 the Battle of Lundy's Lane

the burning of Washington, D.C., by the British on August 24, 1814

When the British invaded Washington in 1814, they burned the books in Congress's library. Thomas Jefferson sold books from his own vast library to replace them. His collection formed the basis for what is now the Library of Congress.

Then, on August 19, British troops landed in Maryland. They **routed** the U.S. forces defending Washington on August 24. President Madison tried to rally the U.S. troops. When defeat appeared certain, he fled. British soldiers dined at the White House that evening before burning it. They also torched the Capitol and destroyed the Library of Congress and other public buildings. Many of Washington's citizens fled before the British arrived. Others remained. Dr. James Ewell saw the flames wrapped around the Capitol. He said that the fire, *"with a noise like thunder, filled all the saddened night with a dismal gloom."*

rout—defeat in a manner that causes disorder

Dolley Madison, the president's wife, remained in the White House most of the day. She had a portrait of George Washington wrapped up and sent to safety. She also saved other White House valuables. Finally, as the British neared the city, she fled. People praised her bravery for staying as long as she did.

Americans were outraged about the destruction of Washington. The British, however, felt they were just doing what U.S. troops had done in York the previous year. Many U.S. citizens blamed their leaders for fleeing. *"Where are our commanders?"* said the *New York Evening Post*. *"Our president and his secretaries are also missing."*

British troops soon withdrew from Washington. They felt as though they had met their goal. Next they tried to capture the key port of Baltimore. Here they met stiffer resistance. British ships bombarded Fort McHenry, which defended the city. But the fort withstood the heavy bombing. Soon after, the British withdrew.

Lawyer and poet Francis Scott Key watched the attack from a British ship. He had gone aboard to seek the release of an American doctor being held captive. Key was not able to leave before the battle began. Key wrote a poem about his thoughts as he saw the fort's flag still flying after almost a full night of bombing. It began, *"O! say can you see, by the dawn's early light, what so proudly we hailed at the twilight's last gleaming…."* The poem was first published under the title *Defence of Fort M'Henry*. It appeared in newspapers up and down the East Coast. Sung to a popular British melody, the song became known as *The Star-Spangled Banner*.

The flag that flew over Fort McHenry during the Battle of Baltimore in 1814 is huge. It measures 30 feet (9 meters) high by 42 feet (12.8 m) long. Its *"broad stripes and bright stars"* inspired Francis Scott Key to write the poem that later became *The Star-Spangled Banner*. The song was named the national anthem in 1931.

THE TIDE TURNS

Britain's failure to capture Baltimore marked a turning point in the war. About the same time, a British force of soldiers and ships invaded New York from Canada. They hoped to capture New York City. This would separate the northern and southern states. The British army clashed with U.S. troops in Plattsburgh, New York. At the same time, British and U.S. ships dueled on nearby Lake Champlain. The battle raged back and forth. Finally U.S. Master Commandant Thomas Macdonough crippled the British flagship, the vessel carrying the commanding officer. *"GLORIOUS NEWS!"* reported a local newspaper. *"The whole of the enemy's FLEET SURRENDERED...."* With their ships defeated, the British foot soldiers retreated as well.

Britain had just ended a long and costly war with France. The British people did not want to face another long war thousands of miles away. *"We might certainly land in different parts of their coast, and destroy some of their towns,"* wrote British Prime Minister Lord Liverpool. *"In the present state of the public mind in America it would be in vain to expect any permanent good effects."*

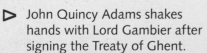
▷ John Quincy Adams shakes hands with Lord Gambier after signing the Treaty of Ghent.

Both sides were tired of fighting. **Diplomats** met in Belgium to negotiate the end of the war. They signed the Treaty of Ghent December 24, 1814. The treaty did not address two key issues that had led to the war. It did not mention the rights of U.S. ships on the open sea or the impressment of U.S. sailors into the British navy. Neither of those issues were still problems, though. Now that the war with France had ended, Britain no longer tried to restrict U.S. trade. And with fewer sailors needed during peacetime, Britain no longer needed to use impressment to get the sailors it needed for its navy.

diplomat—a person who manages a country's affairs with other nations

Timeline of Key Events Relating to the War of 1812

June 1807	British ship *Leopard* fires upon and boards U.S. ship *Chesapeake* in search of deserters from the British Royal Navy. People across the United States are furious.
November 1811	U.S. soldiers under the command of William Henry Harrison defeat American Indian warriors in what is now Indiana.
June 1812	The U.S. declares war on Great Britain.
August 1812	U.S. General William Hull surrenders to British General Isaac Brock at Detroit.
October 1812	A U.S. invasion attempt of Canada fails after defeat at the Battle of Queenston Heights.
April 1813	U.S. troops capture the city of York in Canada.
September 1813	U.S. naval forces defeat the British at the Battle of Lake Erie.
July 1814	The Battle of Lundy's Lane in what is now Niagara Falls, Canada, ends in a bloody draw. It marks the last U.S. attempt to invade Canada.
August 1814	The British capture and burn much of Washington, D.C.
September 1814	U.S. forces win a major victory at the Battle of Plattsburgh in New York. A British attempt to capture Baltimore fails.
December 1814	U.S. and British diplomats agree to end the war through the Treaty of Ghent.
January 1815	U.S. forces led by Andrew Jackson defeat the British at the Battle of New Orleans.
February 1815	The Treaty of Ghent is signed, and the war is declared over.

The treaty did discuss treatment of American Indian tribes. It called on the United States to restore *"all the possessions, rights, and privileges, which they may have enjoyed or been entitled to"* before the war. That didn't happen.

A ship carrying the treaty papers began making its way across the Atlantic Ocean for final approval by the American government. The journey took nearly two months. Meanwhile, the war's most famous battle took place. U.S. forces led by Andrew Jackson with support from pirate Jean Lafitte defeated some of Britain's best soldiers at the Battle of New Orleans on January 8, 1815. In about 30 minutes, roughly 2,000 British troops were killed, wounded, or captured. Newspapers heaped praise on Jackson and his troops. The *Essex Register* cheered the *"splendid victory over the British forces."*

▽   the Battle of New Orleans

After three years of bloody fighting, neither Britain nor the United States had really won anything. Neither side surrendered. No land changed hands. Still both sides felt satisfied. After its wars with France and the United States, Britain finally had peace. The United States, meanwhile, could now focus on expanding into the western frontier. It gained respect from other nations for battling the mighty British to a draw. The United States was a nation on the rise.

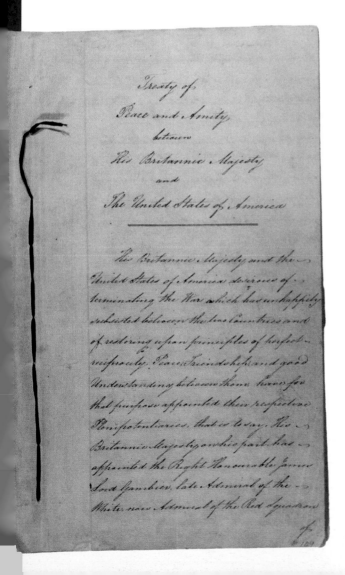

CRITICAL THINKING

In what ways do you think the War of 1812 may have set the stage for westward expansion?

◁ the Treaty of Ghent

SELECTED BIBLIOGRAPHY

Drexler, Kenneth. "A Guide to the War of 1812." U.S. Library of Congress. www.loc.gov/rr/program/bib/1812/

Foreman, Amanda. "The British View the War of 1812 Quite Differently Than Americans Do." Smithsonian.com. www.smithsonianmag.com/history/british-view-war-1812-quite-differently-americans-do-180951852/?page=2

Heidler, David S., and Jeanne T. Heidler. *The War of 1812.* Westport, Conn.: Greenwood Press, 2002.

Taylor, Alan. *The Civil War of 1812: American Citizens, British Subjects, Irish Rebels, & Indian Allies.* New York: Alfred A. Knopf, 2010.

"The Star-Spangled Banner." Smithsonian. amhistory.si.edu/starspangledbanner/

The War of 1812 Website. www.warof1812.ca/battles.htm.

Tucker, Spencer C., and Frank T. Reuter. *Injured Honor: The Chesapeake-Leopard Affair, June 22, 1807.* Annapolis, Md.: Naval Institute Press, 1996.

USS *Constitution* Museum FAQ. www.ussconstitutionmuseum.org/collections-history/faq/

War of 1812. University of Indiana—Bloomington Libraries. http://collections.libraries.iub.edu/warof1812/

GLOSSARY

ally (AL-eye)—a person, group of people, or a country that helps and supports another

annex (an-EKS)—claim authority over the land of another nation

blockade (blok-AYD)—a military effort to keep goods from entering and leaving a region

deserter (di-ZURT-ur)—a military member who leaves duty without permission

diplomat (DI-pluh-mat)—a person who manages a country's affairs with other nations

economy (i-KAH-nuh-mee)—the way a country produces, distributes, and uses its money, goods, natural resources, and services

fleet (FLEET)—a group of ships under a single commander

militia (muh-LISH-uh)—a group of citizens who voluntarily serve as soldiers in emergencies

Parliament (PAHR-luh-muhnt)—the national legislature of Great Britain

port (PORT)—a harbor where ships dock safely

privateer (prye-vuh-TEER)—a private ship that is authorized to attack enemy ships during wartime

restriction (ri-STRIK-shuhn)—a rule or limitation

rout (rowt)—defeat in a manner that causes disorder

INTERNET SITES

FactHound offers a safe, fun way to find Internet sites related to this book. All of the sites on FactHound have been researched by our staff.

Here's all you do:

Visit *www.facthound.com*

Type in this code: 9781491484883

Check out projects, games and lots more at
www.capstonekids.com
Super-cool stuff!

INDEX